GENIUS OPTICAL INVENTIONS

FROM X-RAY TO THE TELESCOPE

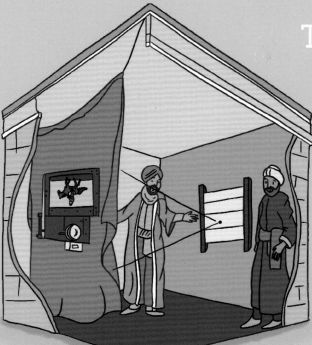

Thanks to the creative team:
Senior Editor: Alice Peebles
Fact Checking: Tom Jackson
Design: www.collaborate.agency

Original edition copyright 2017 by Hungry Tomato Ltd.

Hungry Tomato®
A division of Lerner Publishing Group, Inc.
241 First Avenue North
Minneapolis, MN 55401 USA

For reading levels and more information, look up this title at www.lernerbooks.com.

Main body text set in Josefin Slab SemiBold 10.5/12.
Typeface provided by Font Squirrel.

Library of Congress Cataloging-in-Publication Data

Names: Turner, Matt, 1964- author. | Conner, Sarah, illustrator.
Title: Genius optical inventions : from the X-ray to the telescope / Matt Turner ; illustrated by Sarah Conner.
Description: Minneapolis, MN : Hungry Tomato, a division of Lerner Publishing Group, Inc., [2017] | Series: Incredible inventions | Includes index.
Identifiers: LCCN 2016052520 (print) | LCCN 2017000752 (ebook) | ISBN 9781512432084 (lb : alk. paper) | ISBN 9781512450071 (eb pdf)
Subjects: LCSH: Optical engineering—Juvenile literature. | Optical instruments—Juvenile literature.
Classification: LCC TA1521 .T87 2017 (print) | LCC TA1521 (ebook) | DDC 621.36—dc23

LC record available at https://lccn.loc.gov/2016052520

Manufactured in the United States of America
1-41763-23524-3/7/2017

GENIUS
OPTICAL
INVENTIONS

FROM THE X-RAY TO
THE TELESCOPE

by Matt Turner
Illustrated by Sarah Conner

HUNGRY
TOMATO®

Minneapolis

Galileo (1564-1642) built telescopes to look at objects both close-up and far-off, from insects to planets.

CONTENTS

I love to read by candlelight!

INTO THE LIGHT

When our early ancestors first learned to make fire and control it, they altered human destiny. Now able to make light (and heat), they no longer had to go to bed at sundown. They could stay warm at night and cook food. No more raw meat!

3D projector, 1890s

Eating better food may have even been a trigger that led to our larger brain size, making us more clever. Fire also helped early humans keep pesky bugs and wild beasts at bay. And it helped them hollow out canoes for traveling the oceans and finding new land. Of course, these advances happened a long time ago, and we can't say exactly

Magnifying glass bowl, at least 2,000 years ago

who invented them. They stand more as big leaps forward in human society.

As well as making light, we've learned to focus it through a lens. When humans first polished lenses from rock crystals or used glass globes full of water, they found that these simple lenses could bend light rays and show things magnified, or enlarged. Light is the important bit in microscopes, telescopes, spectacles, and movie cameras.

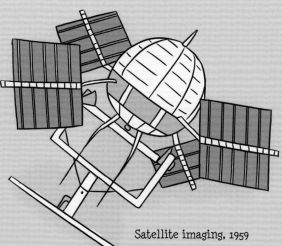

Satellite imaging, 1959

Come with us on a roundabout journey from those early fire-making days to the modern era of lasers and satellite photography. We'll explore some of the more unexpected ways of looking at things—such as radio waves, microwaves, X-rays, and sound waves—which have given us radar and medical scanners.

And we'll poke "light" fun at some of the crazier inventions people have dreamed up . . . such as spectacles for chickens and horses!

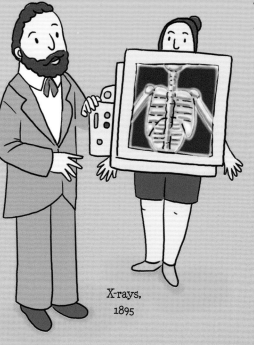

X-rays, 1895

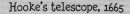

Hooke's telescope, 1665

MAKING LIGHT

You probably have an electric light on right now, don't you? Flicked it on with a switch? Our ancestors weren't so lucky. They used all sorts of tricks, from rubbing sticks together to making matches or giant batteries, all in order to create light.

It's got oil lamp headlights...

FIRE

Around a million years ago, our early ancestors learnt to make fire by rubbing sticks, so creating heat by friction. They also struck sparks from hard stones. Remains of burnt bones show that they cooked meat.

OIL LAMPS

Oil lamps date back more than 12,000 years. They were often made from shells, carved stone, or just a clay cup, and they used animal fat for fuel. Roman lamps ran on olive oil, and some had 10 or 12 wicks each.

LIGHTHOUSES

The Pharos ("light") of Alexandria in Egypt, built over 2,000 years ago, stood nearly 450 ft (137 m) tall, until it was toppled centuries later by earthquakes. A furnace at the top of the Pharos produced the light. Later lighthouses used light bulbs, thanks to Edison's smart idea (right).

MATCHES

The Chinese invented matches about 1,000 years ago, naming them *fire inch sticks*. Reliable friction matches—lit by scraping on sandpaper—first appeared in Britain in the 1820s. These early matches contained phosphorus, which made match factory workers—and sellers, like this boy—very sick.

INCANDESCENT LIGHT

British scientist Humphry Davy invented incandescent light (that is, light resulting from heat) in 1802. He heated a strip of platinum until it glowed, using the world's (then) most powerful battery: 2,000 linked cells. Wow!

I say, do you have this battery in pocket flashlight size?

Hey, I have a great idea...

DAVY'S SAFETY LAMP

Davy is famous for inventing a safety lamp in 1815 to be used by coalminers. Its flame was covered to reduce the risk of gas explosions. It didn't work too well: the light was dim, and the explosions continued. Humph!

EDISON'S GREAT IDEA

American Thomas Edison didn't invent the first light bulb, but in 1879 he came up with the first reliable one—after testing more than 3,000 bulb designs and about 6,000 different filaments! (The filament is the glowing thread inside.)

SEEING NEAR

Magnifying glasses, spectacles, contact lenses, and microscopes all rely on the fact that a curved piece of glass—a lens—focuses light and makes things look closer than they are. Through history, lenses have led to many scientific discoveries (as well as giving us one more thing to lose on the bus).

Carrots, frogs' legs, milk...

MAGNIFIER

Before magnifying glasses existed, the ancient Romans just filled a glass bowl with water. Looking through it, they saw things at larger size.

SPECTACLES

Early Arabs knew about optics, but in the West, English monk Roger Bacon was the first to write about lenses in 1268. Within twenty years, the Italians had invented clip-on specs.

I wish I couldn't see these frogs' legs.

BIFOCALS

American statesman Benjamin Franklin (1706-1790) invented bifocals: glasses with lenses of two different strengths. On a trip to France, he used them to see both his dinner and his fellow diners.

CONTACT LENSES

In 1888, German doctor Adolf Fick designed the earliest practical contact lenses. He first tested them on rabbits. (But how did he know that they worked?!)

How many carrots am I holding up?

ELECTRON MICROSCOPE

Super-powerful scanning electron microscopes (SEMs) were invented in the 1930s by German TV engineer Max Knoll. SEMs were first used to look closely at metals. They also take terrifying pictures of bugs . . .

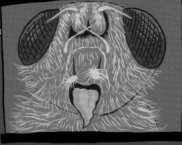

...and this is a house fly's tongue!

Ewww!

Eye piece

Ancient Greek-style water lamp for illumination

Lens barrel

Specimen holder

Focusing ring

HOOKE'S MICROSCOPE

Englishman Robert Hooke was the first to use the word *cell* to describe the basic unit of life. He looked at cells through his microscope in 1665.

SEEING THE INVISIBLE

A microscope uses really powerful lenses to make truly tiny things look big. The first were compound microscopes: tubes with sets of lenses that worked together to magnify. With these, scientists saw bacteria, blood cells, and yeast for the first time. This scope was designed by Dutchman Antonie van Leeuwenhoek (1632-1723). You put a specimen on a sharp point and viewed it through the 275x lens mounted in the plate.

Main screw

Focusing screw

Specimen pin

Objective

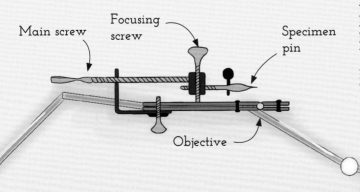

SEEING FAR

Telescopes aren't just for spying on your neighbors. They've enabled astronomers to look deep into space and make discoveries about planets, moons, and stars. Early telescopes used lenses, rather like microscopes, but these days we also use radio telescopes to explore the universe.

EARLY TELESCOPE

Dutchman Hans Lippershey made magnifiers and ran a spectacles shop. In 1608, he came up with an early telescope, which he called a *looker*. He offered it to the government to use in battle, and they promised him a reward if he converted them into binoculars!

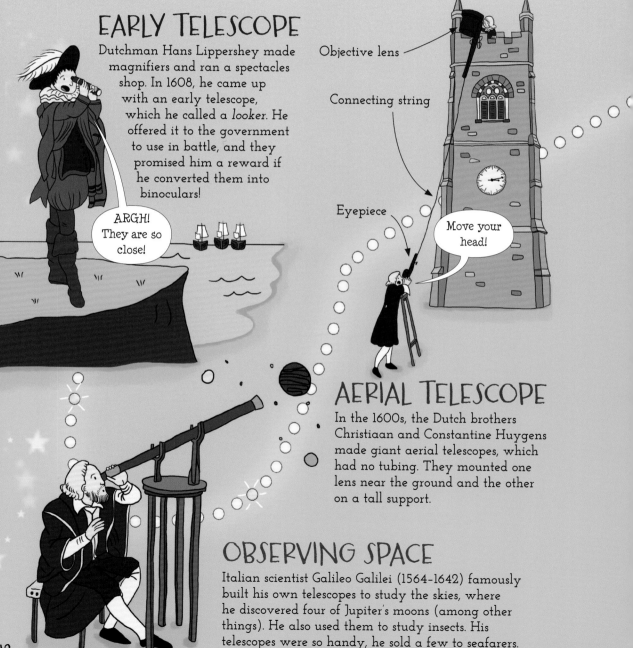

ARGH! They are so close!

Objective lens

Connecting string

Eyepiece

Move your head!

AERIAL TELESCOPE

In the 1600s, the Dutch brothers Christiaan and Constantine Huygens made giant aerial telescopes, which had no tubing. They mounted one lens near the ground and the other on a tall support.

OBSERVING SPACE

Italian scientist Galileo Galilei (1564-1642) famously built his own telescopes to study the skies, where he discovered four of Jupiter's moons (among other things). He also used them to study insects. His telescopes were so handy, he sold a few to seafarers.

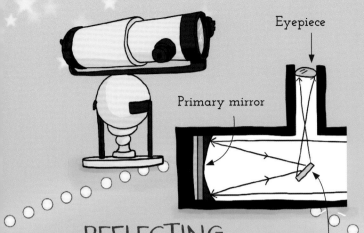

FINDING SATURN'S MOONS

In 1789, German-British astronomer William Herschel built this 40-ft (12-m) long giant. It was a reflecting scope, like Newton's, but with an improved mirror set-up. He used it to look at Saturn's moons. One of them, Mimas, looks scarily like the Death Star . . .

REFLECTING TELESCOPE

Early telescope lenses tended to split light into rainbow colors, making images hard to see. British scientist Isaac Newton fixed this problem in 1668 with a reflecting telescope. This used a mirror, not a lens, to capture the image.

RADIO TELESCOPE

Modern radio telescopes don't look with lenses, but listen like TV antennas. American Karl Jansky built the first radio telescope in a potato field in 1931. He attached antennas to a radio receiver to detect radio waves from space—energy from star activity— which he heard as a steady hiss.

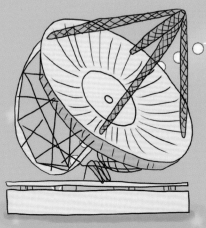

RADIO ASTRONOMY

Jansky's discovery inspired Grote Reber, a fellow American, to build a radio telescope in his back garden in 1937. Reber used it to create a map of space radio signals. In those early years, he was the world's only radio astronomer! These days there are thousands.

THE CAMERA

Cameras are amazingly complex today, but the basic idea comes from the camera obscura (meaning "darkened room"), or pinhole camera. This is a box, with the only light coming from a small hole in one wall. Light enters and, like a film projector, casts an image (upside down) on the opposite wall. If you line that wall with photosensitive film or paper, you capture the image as a photograph.

CAMERA OBSCURA

The Arab scientist Alhazen (965-1040) described how pinhole cameras worked. Astronomers and artists took up the idea.

PHOTOGRAPHIC PAPER PICTURES

Around 1800, British scientist Thomas Wedgwood experimented with photosensitive paper. He left it on sunny windowsills, taking "shadow photos" of leaves and other objects.

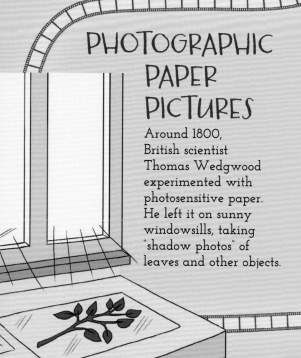

EARLY PHOTOGRAPHY

The true inventors of photography were Frenchmen Nicéphore Niépce and Louis Daguerre. Nic tried photosensitive chemicals (silver chloride, bitumen, lavender oil) and began taking basic photos around 1816. In 1839, Daguerre developed the daguerreotype method. This used a polished silver sheet coated with chemicals and exposed to light in a camera obscura called, yep, a Daguerre (*below*). It took very sharp photographs.

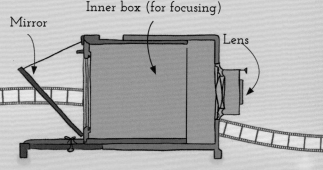

Mirror

Inner box (for focusing)

Lens

Say cheese!

POLAROID PICTURES

The Polaroid camera takes pictures you can instantly print. It was invented in 1947 by American Edwin Land.

DIGITAL CAMERAS

The invention of the charge-coupled device (CCD), an electronic gizmo, by Willard Smith and Bill Boyle in 1969 led to the end of film and the dawn of the digital camera, invented in 1975 by Stephen Sasson.

EASTMAN KODAK

The big revolution in photography came with the invention of film by American George Eastman in 1884. It featured in his Kodak camera, which he patented in 1888. The invention of small, affordable cameras, such as the Brownie, meant that, from then on, anyone could be a photographer.

POSITIVE AND NEGATIVE

Also in the 1830s, British scientist William Fox Talbot came up with the calotype: a better, faster method than the daguerrotype. With the calotype, you could make a negative—a "back to front" image— and use this to make positive copies.

SURVEYING

Surveying means measuring the land. It is important because it gives us maps and GPS (which stops Mom and Dad from getting lost when they're driving). It has also led surveyors on some exciting and dangerous journeys.

MEASURING MOUNTAINS

Ancient Egyptians used long, knotted ropes for measuring distances. Early Chinese (below) used a protractor on a pole to calculate mountain heights by measuring angles. This method, or versions of it, was used for manycenturies.

I'm sure it's around here somewhere...

FIRST MAP

Here is the first known map of the world: the Imago Mundi from Babylon (in modern-day Iraq). An unknown person scratched it onto a clay tablet some 2,500 years ago. The ring represents the ocean surrounding the land.

SATELLITE IMAGING

These days, satellites orbiting Earth take photos so clear, they can spot you sunbathing in the garden. Explorer 6, launched in 1959, took some of the first photos from space. They were very fuzzy, but it was the dawn of satellite imaging.

THEODOLITES

To chart new empires, surveyors went out with theodolites. These were basically telescopes that measured angles very accurately. Some were huge, like this one built by Jesse Ramsden in England in the 1780s, weighing nearly 22 lb (100 kg). And in the early United States, the young George Washington was the first surveyor of northern Virginia . . .

AERIAL PHOTOGRAPHY

Frenchman Nadar launched aerial photography in 1858. This was his biggest balloon, named The Giant. He also invented airmail! During 1870–1871, he used a fleet of balloons to smuggle more than two million messages out of Paris, which was under siege by the Germans.

RECONNAISSANCE

Maul's "rocket-cam" never really took off because aerial photographers were using planes. First off was Wilbur Wright (pioneer of flight), in 1909. In World War I, enemy positions were recorded in this way by both sides.

I hope I remembered the film!

ROCKET CAMERAS

Swedish genius Alfred Nobel (famous for the Nobel Prize) pioneered aerial photography from rockets in 1897. In 1906, German engineer Albert Maul (*right*) built a more efficient design, powered by compressed air.

MAKING MOVIES

Who doesn't love watching movies? Your great-great-grandparents, that's who. After all, the film camera is still quite young, having first appeared in the 1890s. But long before then, inventors had begun to make clever toys that tricked our eyes into thinking we were looking at moving pictures . . . movies.

PHENAKISTOSCOPE

One toy was the phenakistoscope of 1832, invented by Belgian Joseph Plateau. It had two discs, one ringed with pictures. You spun the discs, looked through a slot at a mirror, and saw the pictures "join up" and appear to move.

ZOOPRAXISCOPE

Similar toys included the zoopraxiscope (Eadweard Muybridge, 1879). It made the first moving photographic image.

FIRST MOVIE CAMERA

Some claim that Thomas Edison invented the movie camera—but the true pioneer was France's Louis Le Prince. He used this camera (*right*) to shoot some film in Leeds, England, in 1888. Two years later he disappeared, so he never got rich from his invention.

Come on— hurry up!

KINETOGRAPH

Edison and his helper Bill Dickson did invent a movie camera called the Kinetograph. And in 1891, he unveiled the Kinetoscope projector, which showed movies. But only one person could use it at a time.

VCR TECHNOLOGY

In modern times you can watch movies on a smartphone. A generation ago, your mom and dad watched them with a VCR, which is short for video cassette recorder. The first VCR was made by Russian-American Alex Poniatoff and his Ampex company. It was so huge, you couldn't even carry it, let alone tuck it in your pocket.

MOVIEMAKERS

The first true moviemakers were French brothers Auguste and Louis Lumière. In 1895, they filmed their workers leaving the factory, then gave a public screening of—guess what they called it?—*Workers Leaving the Lumière Factory*. It sounds deadly boring, but viewers were amazed (even though these first films had no sound at all).

VIEWING IN 3D

Movies in 3D are great fun. But they, like the old phenakistoscope, are simply clever tricks that fool your brain. You might think that making and viewing three-dimensional pictures is new, but it's more than 150 years old—even older than the movie camera.

STEREOSCOPE

3D pictures date back almost to the invention of photography. The Brewster Stereoscope of 1849 held two photos—left and right—each taken from a slightly different spot. Viewed together, they gave a 3D effect.

Eyepiece

Wahoo!

3D PROJECTOR

Alfred Molteni, an Italian-French optician, used a special slide projector with two lenses to create a 3D effect. This audience is watching his nature slides.

Ahh!

CINERAMA

A more modern, movie version of Molteni's rig was Cinerama, invented by American Fred Waller. It used a huge, curved cinema screen, with a "joined-up" picture created by three film projectors. At the first viewing in 1952, people were so excited, they screamed! But Cinerama was hopelessly complicated and expensive until they worked out a way of using just one projector.

3D SCANNING

In 1859 at the circular studio of François Willème in Paris, you had your picture taken by twenty-four cameras mounted around the wall. Willème used a projector to copy each photo outline to a lump of clay, then carved it into a 3D *photosculpture*. So 3D scanning and printing was born.

I love being the center of attention!

SPECIAL EFFECTS

The modern version of Willème's rig, as used in the movie industry, is called photogrammetry. Digital cameras take lots of scans of an actor, then animators use these to create the special effects that you watch at the movies.

APP SCAN

123D Catch, created in 2009 by Autodesk, takes 3D scans of objects, which can then be tinkered with on a computer and even 3D-printed. Willème would have loved it!

SCANNING THE BODY

So far we've looked at bacteria, outer space, planet Earth. Now it's time to look inside the body. Sounds gross? Maybe–but it saves millions of lives. These days, it's called radiography, or radiology, because it uses the types of radiation wave that can pass through our bodies. Radiographers can also use sound waves to take pictures of our insides.

EARLY ENDOSCOPE

Around 1800, German doctor Philipp Bozzini invented his light conductor. It had a candle and lens for looking right inside an ear or throat. It was one of the first endoscopes.

Oh my!

X-RAYS IN BATTLE

Scientists soon realized X-rays could be lifesavers. Polish-French chemist Marie Curie was a brilliant radiologist. During World War 1, she sent special medical trucks to the battlefields to take X-rays of wounded soldiers. She won many awards for her studies on radioactivity.

FIRST X-RAY

In Germany in 1895, Wilhelm Röntgen discovered that certain rays could pass straight through cardboard onto a screen where they glowed. He took the first X-ray photograph, showing the bones in his wife Anna's hand.

CT SCANNER

Computerized tomography (CT) scanners, which look a bit like giant donuts, photograph the body slice by slice. English engineer Godfrey Hounsfield invented it in the early 1970s. He tested it first on a dead human brain, then a cow's brain—then on himself!

Umm... cheese?

MRI

Armenian-American Raymond Damadian created MRI, or magnetic resonance imaging. In 1977, Ray showed that by measuring what happens to the potassium inside us when it is energized, a scanner can "see" cancer tumours. Each year, radiologists take over 60 million MRI scans, helping to save countless lives.

Ray's original sketch for an MRI machine looked a bit like this.

ULTRASOUND

Ian Donald and Tom Brown invented ultrasound in the 1950s for checking ships for flaws. In modern times, it's used for checking babies before they're born.

PILLCAM

Digital cameras are now so tiny, you can even swallow one in a pill! The PillCam can spot problems in our gut as it passes through the digestive system. It was invented in 1997 by Israeli Gavriel Iddan. He learned his skills by working on guided missiles— rockets that find their own way to a target.

Pillcam

23

SONAR AND RADAR

Sonar is short for **so**und **n**avigation **a**nd **r**anging. It is a technology we've borrowed from nature. It creates pictures from sound waves as they echo off objects—like a bat catches moths or a dolphin catches fish. Radar also picks up echoes, but it uses radio waves instead of sound.

SONAR EXPERIMENT

In 1822, Daniel Colladon and Charles Sturm used gunpowder and bells in a Swiss lake to measure how fast sound traveled in water. (It's four times faster than in air.) This was arguably the first sonar.

DISASTER AT SEA

In 1912, more than 1,500 passengers and crew died when the *Titanic* ocean liner sank. Experts later realized that if the ship had been fitted with sonar, it would likely have seen the iceberg in its path and avoided it.

Chain Home radio masts

WARTIME RADAR

Scotsman Robert Watson-Watt helped develop radar (**ra**dio **d**etection **a**nd **r**anging) into a war-winning technology. It was first used to help pilots detect thunderstorms.

Just before World War II, Watson-Watt proved that aircraft themselves could reflect radio waves. At his suggestion, Britain set up radar defences on the coast, called Chain Home, for detecting enemy aircraft up to 60 miles (96 km) away.

ICE DEVICE

Canadian engineer Reginald Fessenden designed a sonar system that could detect icebergs up to 2 miles (1.2 km) away, measure the sea's depth and send messages by Morse code. His invention was later fitted to submarines.

MAPPING THE SEABED

In modern times, sonar helps ships detect the seabed, even though it lies far below them in total darkness. They use it to study rock formations and also to spot shipwrecks or sunken planes. This ship is using multibeam sonar, which sends out a fan-shaped signal. Echoes from the signal describe the shape of the sea floor.

Ice sea you clearly.

PROXIMITY FUSE

Another wartime secret weapon used by the Allies was the proximity fuse. It was a kind of radar fitted into the tip of a shell fired from a gun. Radiation waves detected a target (such as a plane in the air), which made the shell explode.

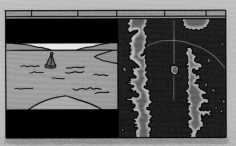

NAVIGATION AID

These days, radar is widely used for peaceful purposes, such as guiding ships at night. A ship's microwave radar scanner sends out radio waves and picks up reflections from solid structures, which show up on screen.

LASER LIGHT

If you've made it this far in the book, you're doing well. Let's face it, light is complicated stuff. And now we get to the really tricky subject: lasers! We use lasers every day—in CD and DVD players, for instance, and laser printers and laser displays. So who invented them, and how do they work?

MEET THE PHOTONS

To understand lasers, it helps to know a bit about light. Light is electromagnetic radiation—like a visible cousin of the invisible X-ray. In 1905, German scientist Albert Einstein described light as made up of tiny bits called photons, often shown as squiggles: wave-packets.

HOW A LASER WORKS

At the center of a laser is a cylinder filled with a gain medium: a gas or crystal. At each end of the cylinder is a mirror with a small hole. The gain medium is "pumped" with electricity or with light energy (photons). The photons excite the gain medium, which gives out more photons. Eventually, the photons fire out from the end of the laser.

LASER BUILDERS

The first working laser was built in 1960 by Theodore Maiman in the United States. But he couldn't have done it without the pioneering work of other scientists in the United States, Russia, and Iran in the 1950s. Some of them are shown below.

Charles Townes

Arthur Schawlow

Gordon Gould

Ali Javan

SUPER-CUTTER

Lasers, once described as "a solution looking for a problem," are used in all sorts of devices these days. A cutting laser, for instance, will cut metal, wood, and fabric. It can cut anything from very thin, delicate parts up to 0.5-in-thick (12-mm-thick) steel. The cutting pattern is computer-guided.

My lidar is faster than your car...

LIDAR GUN

Police use lidar guns to check on unsafe driving. Lidar works a bit like radar but uses laser light instead of radio waves. It is super-accurate, homing in on a single car and gauging the speed in a split-second. If you see one pointing at your car, tell your parents to slow down . . .

LASER BROOM

One of the dangers facing astronauts is the growing amount of space junk: bits of old spacecraft orbiting Earth at high speed. One speck of metal hitting your spacecraft could cause a catastrophe! One day, NASA may use laser brooms: Earth-based laser weapons that could zap the junk and push it out of harm's way.

CRAZY INVENTIONS

BOILED PEE

The grandfather of the glow stick, which is basically a chemical light, was German chemist Hennig Brand. In 1669, Hennig boiled a flask of his pee until it caught fire and turned into glowing phosphorus (the chemical that was later used in matches). Nice!

HORSE SENSE

The Dollond family of London were famous for inventing lenses for telescopes and spectacles, but in 1893 they went one step further when Mr. Dollond invented bifocal glasses for horses. Why? The glasses made the road surface seem closer than it was, causing the horse to walk in a high-stepping manner (which was thought attractive in those days). Apparently, the horses enjoyed wearing them.

SPECS, NOT PECKS

It's not just horses, either! In 1903, American Andrew Jackson invented tiny pairs of glasses, or spectacles, for farm chickens to wear. His aim was to stop them pecking each other, as this made them sick. The specs were primarily eye protectors and were rose-tinted to stop the hens becoming more frantic at the sight of blood, and pecking more. Jackson's idea worked.

LIEUTENANT PIGEON

Remember those aerial photographers? Well, in 1908, Dr. Julius Neubronner of Germany invented a miniature camera . . . for pigeons. Strapped to the bird's chest, it worked by means of a timer, which went off regularly. He showed it off at public fairs, where people could buy postcards of pics taken by the birds. Later, Neubronner's pigeon camera was used in World War I. Crazy, but true.

LOOKING AROUND CORNERS

Hamblin glasses, invented in the 1930s, were special specs that reflected light at a 45-degree angle. They allowed you to lie flat on your back (if, say, you were sick or tired) but still read from a book resting on your chest. If that sounds appealing, you're in luck: you can still buy them online!

LIGHT-HEADED

Since the nineteenth century, solar baths had been a popular "cure" for diseases of the head, such as a snotty nose or earache. This model is from the 1930s: patients put their head inside the big can, where an ultraviolet ray-gun fired artificial sunlight at it. UV light makes vitamin D, which is good for your body—but it also fries your skin and can cause cancers, which is not so good.

ANTI-AIRCRAFT TUBAS

These things look like a monstrous brass band, but they're actually giant ear trumpets. Armies used them in both world wars to listen for the engines of approaching enemy aircraft. When Robert Watson-Watt developed radar, war-tubas were no longer needed.

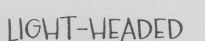

DAFT AND DEFT PREDICTIONS

THE ELECTRIC LIGHT BULB

Back in the 1870s–1880s, when Thomas Edison was working on his light bulb idea, lots of people reckoned it would never work. Here are some of the daft things they said:

"Everyone acquainted with the subject will recognize it as a conspicuous failure." —Henry Morton, president of the Stevens Institute of Technology

"When the Paris Exhibition closes, electric light will close with it and no more will be heard of it." —Oxford professor Erasmus Wilson, 1888

"The electric light has no future." —British inventor John Pepper

SWITCHED ON

Despite his gloomy (and obviously way wrong) prediction, Pepper was a huge fan of electricity. He used arc lamps to light up Trafalgar Square and St Paul's Cathedral in London for the wedding of Edward, Prince of Wales, and Alexandra of Denmark in 1863. He also invented a way of projecting a "ghost" of an actor onto the stage. It was so clever, even the brilliant scientist Michael Faraday begged him to explain how it was done.

Not so cleverly, when visiting Australia in the very dry summer of 1882, Pepper tried to make rain by firing big naval guns and rockets at the sky. It failed, and everyone laughed at him, so he gave up.

YES, IT DID COME TRUE...

Some people were better at making predictions. In his 1863 novel *Paris in the Twentieth Century*, French writer Jules Verne made several accurate predictions for the year 1960:

★ cities with electric lighting
★ skyscrapers
★ high-speed trains
★ a global message network (rather like the Internet)
★ fax machines
★ cars
★ the electric chair (eek!)
★ weapons of mass destruction (boo!)

Amazingly, his publisher, Mr. Hetzel, thought the story was too boring, so it was never published in Verne's lifetime.

SIMON SAYS

Astrologers study star charts and the zodiac to predict the future. They are sometimes wrong. Astronomers are very different: they are space scientists. But sometimes they, too, make mistakes.

In ancient Greece, Aristotle suggested that the sun circled Earth. And later on, Ptolemy backed him up. We now know, of course, that it's the other way around: the planets in our solar system orbit the sun.

More recently, in 1898, Canadian-American astronomer Simon Newcomb said, "We are probably nearing the limit of all we can know about astronomy." After a few more years' study, Simon wisely changed his mind, calling astronomy "an illimitable field."

INDEX

The Author

British-born Matt Turner graduated from Loughborough College of Art in the 1980s, since then he has worked as a picture researcher, editor, and writer. He has authored books on diverse topics, including natural history, earth sciences, and railways, as well as hundreds of articles for encyclopedias and partworks, covering everything from elephants to abstract art. He and his family currently live near Auckland, Aotearoa/New Zealand, where he volunteers for the local Coastguard unit and dabbles in art and craft.

The Illustrator

Sarah Conner lives in the lovely English countryside, in a cute cottage with her dogs and a cat. She spends her days sketching and doodling the world around her. She has always been inspired by nature and it influences much of her work. Sarah formerly used pens and paint for her illustrations, but in recent years she has transferred her style to the computer as it better suits today's industry. However, she still likes to get her watercolors out from time to time and paint the flowers in her garden!